Homecoming

Homecoming

— *poems* —

Kay Mullen

*The time is now — The stories, the listening
Warmest wishes,
Kay Mullen*

FITHIAN PRESS, MCKINLEYVILLE, CALIFORNIA, 2019

Copyright © 2019 by Kay Mullen
All rights reserved
Printed in the United States of America

The interior design and the cover design of this book are intended for and limited to the publisher's first print edition of the book and related marketing display purposes. All other use of those designs without the publisher's permission is prohibited.

Published by Fithian Press
A division of Daniel and Daniel, Publishers, Inc.
Post Office Box 2790
McKinleyville, CA 95519
www.danielpublishing.com

Distributed by SCB Distributors (800) 729-6423

LIBRARY OF CONGRESS CATALOGING-IN-PUBLICATION DATA
Names: Mullen, Kay, author.
Title: Homecoming : poems / by Kay Mullen.
Description: McKinleyville, California : Fithian Press, 2019.
Identifiers: LCCN 2019007322 | ISBN 9781564746139 (pbk. : alk. paper)
Classification: LCC PS3613.U446 A6 2019 | DDC 811/.6—dc23
LC record available at https://lccn.loc.gov/2019007322

Dedicated to
all who love and protect children

ACKNOWLEDGMENTS

I'm grateful to the following publications where these poems first appeared, some with minor changes.

Appalachia Journal of Mountaineering & Conservation: "Wood Path," "Woods Near Lake Elysian," "Salt," "Sandpipers," "For What They Are," "A Wild Order," "Mt. Rainier," "In Ragged Tide Waters." "The Pond" will appear in the spring/summer issue, 2019.

Avocet, A Journal of Nature Poetry: "Woman Feeding Birds," "A Hammock."

Carquinez Poetry Review: "Flycatcher."

Catholic Things: anthology edited by Janet McCann, Texas A & M University. "In Bas-relief," "Hidden Mystics."

Crosswinds Poetry Journal: "Away."

Dancing at the Edges: Poems by the Fusion Collective: "Clara," "In the Optician's Waiting Room." "A Case for Lightning," previously published by *San Pedro River Review*, "Closet Door," "The Honey Work of Bees" previously published by *Valparaiso Poetry Review*, "Midwest Storm," previously published by *Wrist Magazine*.

Floating Bridge Review Pontoon: "Between Cemetery Road and the Blue Tavern," previously published in *Sisters Today*.

In Tahoma's Shadow: Poems from the City of Destiny: "Accordion Boy."

Minotaur: "The Holly Tree."

Mute Note Earthward: Washington State Poets: "A Thread."

On Becoming: What Makes a Woman, University of Nebraska Press: "House in Hopkinton."

Poetry Therapy: "Snow Blind." An earlier version of "Black Trunk" appeared in my book *Let Morning Begin* under the title "Weathered Trunk."

San Pedro Poetry Review: "A Case for Lightning," later published in *Dancing at the Edges: Poems by the Fusion Collective.*

Shark Reef Literary Journal: "First Visit," "In Praise of Skunk Cabbage," "Snow Goose," "As If We'd Walked Through Fire Together."

Switched-on Guttenberg: "Ghetto Cemetery."

Third Wednesday, A Quarterly Journal of Literary and Visual Arts: "In Celebration of Telephone Wires."

20/20: Tacoma In Images and Verse: The Photography of Peter Serko: "Stone Wall", "More Than."

Valparaiso Poetry Review: "Who Knows," "Sidewalk Artist," "An Dinh Palace," "Up Close." The poems "Closet Door" and "The Honey Work of Bees," later published in *Dancing at the Edges: Poems by the Fusion Collective*.

Wrist Magazine: "Midwest Storm," later published in *Dancing at the Edges: Poems by the Fusion Collective*.

My deepest thanks to Holly Hughes, who gave me the incentive to write these words and who guided me through this work to completion. Her support, encouragement and insights sustained me each step of the way. I'm grateful to Janet McCann for her close look at various poems and her insightful comments. My thanks also to the Fusion poets of Olympia for their critiques of many of these poems, and to the Inscape poets of Catherine Place whose support to carry on has been invaluable. Gratitude is also due to mentors and teachers at Hugo House and the University of Washington for grounding me in the world of poetry. I thank the staff, my mentors and colleagues at Pacific Lutheran University for their motivation and vision. Thanks also to my editor, John Daniel, for his guidance and careful attention to details in all phases of the publishing process, and to Kathleen Flenniken, Allen Braden and Edward Byrne for their affirmation of my work. I want to thank the Sisters of St. Francis, who launched me into a major phase of my personal growth, for their trust and lasting friendships. I will always be grateful for my husband, Anthony, who understood and loved me unconditionally, and my two sons, whose love continues to encourage and affirm my writing efforts. Finally, thanks to all—too numerous to mention—who helped me bring this work to completion.

Contents

To the Reader 17

I. What Passes Through
    First Visit 21
    What Passes Through 22
    Singer 23
    Wash Day 24
    Fall Ritual 25
    Black Trunk 26
    Stone Wall 28
    Silence the Daily Bread 29
    A Woman Dances 30
    A Thread 31
    Snow Blind 32
    Consider the Possible 33
    Summer Storm 34
    A Case for Lightning 35
    The Letter 36
    Gone Before 37
    The Back Road Ahead 38
    You Ask How 39
    To Saint Francis 40
    Survivor 41

II. A Road Rarely Taken
    Arrivals 45
    The House in Hopkinton 46
    As If We'd Walked Through Fire Together 48
    Clara 49

Summer Days 50
A Road Rarely Taken 52
Up Close 54
The Clapboard House 55
Invisible Questions 56
The Woman from India Who Lives Across the Street 57
Ahimsa Women 58
In Bas-relief 59
Hidden Mystics 60
Sidewalk Artist 61
Mahsi 62
Art Gallery Karma 63
In the Optician's Waiting Room 64
Refuge 65
Who Knows 66

III. A Wild Order

The Honey Work of Bees 69
Even Pebbles 70
Flycatcher 71
In Celebration of Telephone Wires 72
Between Cemetery Road and the Blue Tavern 73
Autumn Zen 74
A Wild Order 75
Woman Feeding Birds 76
The Holly Tree 77
A Hammock 78
Sandpipers 79
Wood Path 80
Salt 81
In Praise of Skunk Cabbage 82
The Pond 83
Snow Goose 84

For What They Are 85
Mount Rainier 86
In Ragged Tide Waters 87
Woods Near Lake Elysian 88
More Than 89

IV. The Country of Home
   Away 93
   Returning Home 94
   Feasts on the Mekong Delta 95
   An Dinh Palace 96
   Topiary 97
   Souvenirs 98
   Ebbingstraat 99
   Under a Prague Moon 100
   Art Gallery 102
   At a Kiosk in Prague Square 103
   Ghetto Cemetery 105
   Karlovy Vary 106
   On a Train from Padua to Venice 107
   Pigeons Roosting on Ledges of the
      Bank Building and Loan 108
   Poor Man 109
   From One Instant Reflection to the Next 110
   Town Clock 111
   A Home to Remember 112
   Answers 113
   Lasting 115

Homecoming

To the Reader

Before engaging the muse, consider.
It will not let you go unless you give up.
Ideas and objects may be lonely affairs
yet once engaged they lift you out of yourself

into unknowns: a stunned silence
at the summit's magenta dusk, beach winds
that whip the lines of your face
at a sunset's fascination. Be prepared.

Find a country of quiet, a de facto friend
who will nod and say yes. After
you spend enough time emptying fruitless
hours of the day, sit with yourself on a lonely

bench. The muse will find you no matter
what park you choose, or chair. She will turn
your chin to the blue, ask what you see
in the fleeting breeze of a cloud, a cottonwood

with its summer snow, a hummingbird egg
the size of a bean. When you find a link
to the world, one that makes your fingers
quiver like feathers, your mind race

with pelicans flying in formation, or where
a final strand fastens a silver web, then ink
and words open summits of mountains and sky,
places you never intended your words to go.

I. What Passes Through

All language is a longing for home.

—*The Essential Rumi*
translated by Coleman Barks
with John Moyne

First Visit

A child of eight remembers the narrow
rutted road, dust swirling behind a gray sedan.
Around a bend, wild roses climb
a wrought-iron gate. Seven years her mother
lies beside loved ones enduring as oak shade

in August, yellow leaves like fragile letters
tucked away in a locked trunk.
Hand-me-down memories linger from wall
hangings and hushed tones overheard,
torn music sheets flattened

on a secret shelf of the secretary, initialed
linens never used. Refrains still sing
from fingers that once flew over the keys
like wings, her brush strokes: the misty lake,
the fields of lupine, the cabin smoke.

What Passes Through

A prism hangs from my kitchen window.
Refracted light scatters
        through the room, illumines
space with rainbow gleams.

On the way into town,
a gem dangles from a cord
in a passing car, flashing colors
        as the crystal pivots.

Pinpoints of jewels, unspoken
gems fill reserves of the day
        the way ideas pass through
a cut-glass pitcher, a parliament
of owls, a carved panther.

What passes through may not
be light. Silence
        may cloak a room
with a dark no one can see

        a match spark, a candle flame.
When light of dreams cannot find
a way, hopes dissolve,
        the search may die.

Singer

My mother chooses blue material
from Brown's Department Store. After
school and on weekends she sits beside
the steel wheel of her Singer sewing
machine, pumping on the pedals in silence.

I look forward to fittings of the coat
when she softly touches me with the flat
of her hand across my shoulders
and arms. With pins in a cushion, she folds
the hem with careful measure.

Sometimes at night when an owl flies low
from the alley barn and the house
hushes from the flurry of day,
she attaches buttons and pockets.

When the special morning finally arrives,
I wear my new coat with a Sunday pride,
Easter clothing me with a touch of light
I never want to go out. I can still
hear that singing machine, though
the fabric of our lives seemed frayed.

Wash Day

Summer Mondays my mother rises early to fill
the galvanized tubs, steam rising from her weekly
stew. She calls me when first sheets stiffen through
rubber rollers, then fold into a basket on the concrete
floor like taffy at the county fair. She stirs the sudsy
mix with a wooden rod, aprons and towels churning
in hot suds. From rinse to final rinse, she swings
the wringer above the wicker basket. After the last
wrinkle of white weaves out, we each grasp one wire
handle and balance our way up basement stairs
like mute Sherpas breathing hard into sultry air.

Outside, we pass each other wiping parallel lines
like paths of our lives, familiar, silent and certain.
Wind blows its breath through the garments as if
a dance could rise from flapping shirts and flannels
as they gyrate on the lines. Yet the work matters,
the march of duties across the day. We snatch
clothespins from a cloth bag, stuff extras between
our teeth until white ghosts billow, underclothes
invisible as if our inner lives can never be revealed,
as if we could always keep them secret. The first load
of wash safely pinned, we descend again to the damp
basement. The work unravels its own voice, leads us
through our own thoughts. *I miss the wash
of her paintings, music sheets no longer turned,
lines and spaces unnoted.* All morning soapy water
sloshes, the steady drone goes on and on
as if the rhythm of Mondays will never change.

Fall Ritual

It was an annual street thing, the fire
my father supervised, our garden potatoes
planted in a huge pile of autumn leaves.

When he struck the match to a crisp leaf
the fire leapt and snapped. We stepped back
from the swirling smoke cloud whirling

in plumes down Linden Street. When the last
bushels of leaves were thrown to the flames,
we waited for ashes to slowly cook

our main dish to a tender doneness.
A bicycle ride around the block, a game
of tag until time to gather the spuds with tongs.

Father carried the bowl to the kitchen table.
I can still hear the crackling flames, feel
the heat, taste the smoked potatoes

steaming with butter still on my tongue—
remember that once-in-an-autumn feast,
the ashes littering my empty plate.

Black Trunk

The house next door would fit
our family, my father said.
When we moved he let us explore
the spare room, twelve
spice drawers at the bottom

of the stairs, and mirrored closet
at the end of the hall, but not
a black trunk he strapped
and stored in the barn garage.
It sat in front of the Ford's

steel fenders, was locked
and not to be teased with any key.
Though never stated,
clearly understood. No questions
raised. For years we stacked
summer screens, storm
windows, fed and watered

the few chickens in the attached
coop, walked past the fish pond
to the back door
and never bothered
the black trunk. As a child,
I guessed it belonged to *her*,
my mother who died of a fever.

I imagined it held her diary,
ecru lace or the pearls in the picture
my grandmother gave me to keep
her memory alive. Did it contain
soft shoes and sheet music, paintings

between onion paper, dried petals?
When I finally left as a young adult
and returned to a house
in another part of town,
the black trunk had vanished.

I wondered if my father feared
the content of talk he refused
to express, to open what he kept
hidden inside of himself, and
in the heart of that trunk
where it beat until he died.

Stone Wall
Chalk Girl of Frost Park

An artist chalks her in place, creates
her image on stone. She can't be more
than five, apparent loneliness pocked

with neglect. This is the confused child
who can't find her place, can't be heard
for who she is. Winds and bitter rains

may wear her away until only a memory
remains. From a tiny window, a light
shines small as a candle flame

like a kind word to summon her, to lift
her gently to the ground, to shake the dust
from her heart and quicken

her breath again. There, something bright
on the green incline, summer grass
and trees the color of forgiveness.

Silence the Daily Bread

> *The penalty for silence is loss.*
> —Colette Inez, *Clemency*,
> "My Father and the Lord of Null"

All that remains, a photo, he staring ahead
as if seeing himself in a mirror, she, holding

her first born, eyes lowered. Years later
the aunt reveals the wedding day's need.

Her sister bears three daughters, the youngest
not the father's hoped-for son. A year later,

a marked grave, a mother's battle lost, three
children left. Deafening secrecy spreads

a cloud. Doors close, questions never
rise, silence the daily bread. Years later

a son leaves home, marries, never returns.
Another looses a chance. At last, one inches

over the edge of her life, and
in a breath of clarity discovers light.

All loving words lost in a daily silence.

A Woman Dances

on the dining room wall.
She is at home
on the tapestry with castanets,
banjos and flutes. Her scarves
flow in the silky rhythm
of violins while the crowd sways
and claps on a sunny afternoon.
Mothers hold infants.
Fathers lift the children.

A family sits at a table
in silence, the rituals predictable.
Is the tapestry only a piece of art
to cover the emptiness, to fill
the chill of vacant space
like a room with only one chair?

The only sounds, the tinkle
of utensils, the tick of plates.
No one notices a holiday
on the wall. No one speaks
out of turn, though, for a moment
a child at the table might
thread a daring thought, break
a strand of silence with a word,
a thrum of fingers,
the almost audible
hum of a tune.

A Thread

                    must be thin
and strong to pass through an eye,
the point of entry clean and decisive,
no fuzzy ends, no hair of excess.

                    Once
through the narrow way,
who can say where the seams will go
in the light and all the unknowns.
Let the hand that weaves the needle

stitch a coat to keep out the cold,
           keep in the warmth,
a garment that breathes in the sun.

                    Even a man
could pass through an eye if he bends
and is willing to see himself as a web
                    in the world,
if humble enough to believe,

though he dangles by a strand
                over a deep ravine.

Snow Blind

Father, word I had no meaning for, your eyes
screening me invisible, ears deaf, voiceless.
My found words finally ask from what
ancestral glacier did you flow, wedge
out of reach of warm winds, splintered floe
shattering our innocent years? Forced upward,
snow banks blocked finally collapse.

You, snow-blind, we, your young
in eye of storm, unbonded like powdered bits
sprawled across wide fields of endless white.
Stiffened under hard-pack, cold quickened
our hearts like chinks in igloos we shaped
as children, hands stinging and toes,
mittens crisp with snow beads waiting
like tears for a warm hearth.

Now you are old, refusing to leave
the mountain. I have called across crevasses,
thrown ropes you've wrapped,
like frozen cables crushing, ice flow
that could have wound its way downstream
to where I wait for thaw to fill
your emptiness with spring. I wait,
and in the waiting—fill my own.

Consider the Possible

                        To discover
step away, take a telescopic approach or see

with the naked eye when the moon appears
        as a white globe.
                        Imagine
spherical phases, the circular measure of earth
and sea from afar.

Consider
        a sky full of pinpoint stars and ring-shaped
planets. Even sun with its fiery fields appears

on the horizon, a silent sphere surrounded
by blazes of sunset.   Amazing orbs

speak to the shape of O's like eyes of the living,
like rings we place on committed fingers,

        or balls of words we toss to each other
as we covet the bowl of acceptance,

seek the possible bound in circles,
        a deep sense of belonging.

Summer Storm

Breezes ripple weeds
for days, begin to quicken, slacken
the reins of galloping clouds.

Far-off lightning flickers.
Between thunder rolls, light snaps
the sky, gusts whip the flagstone

walls, race through hollows
of the bell tower. In the distance
a low rumble as if a funnel swirls

across the drenched fields,
everything in its path whirled
in the tempest. Rain sheets

the window. I close the drapes
as if I could blanket the noise,
as if shards of lightning would cease

to brighten the walls and bounce
from the mirror. Another siege
to be endured, to run its course like

all rage does. As quickly as the chaos
swells, earth swivels a notch,
the storm rolls over the horizon,

turns the knob of its spent door
to a scene of calm, wet macadam
steaming like morning horses.

A Case for Lightning

Sit with a storm
raging outside your window.

Don't cover
your ears at thunderclaps

or close your eyes
to white streaks

snapping the clouds.
Let the rumbles roll

over your head like heartbeats.
Let lightning ricochet across

the sky and run its course.
Then you will know

what before the storm
you could not understand.

The Letter

One more loss.
Soon words fill a room
with a frightening dark. Yet,

somewhere a small door
opens to surprise me
at the last moment, and

like a thrush, I fly through.
It is true, this bird
of belief clinging

to a thistle branch can see
with a third eye. I grieve,
not my loss,
        but yours.

Gone Before

A coffin closes.
The procession down the aisle
begins with all the questions,
the unfinished life and death decisions

sealed in white satin and a woman
who can no longer hear
or grasp what I needed to say.

My mind numb,
grieving abandoned years ago
for even a brief sign of awareness
like rain returning to clouds.

My thoughts retreat to the river
dividing the town with rushing
      that waits for no one.

The Back Road Ahead

It's back around the bends, beyond
farms where Angus graze, soybean fields,

silos, sheds and sagging barns. Back
to where it all began: the town, the street,

the house. No need to walk or find. Instead
explore that place of mind to sense and sort,

see the past from new emerging places
apart where facing and finding has a chance.

The *it*, a shift of eye, a quick hand, a tone
of voice, daily dismissals, silence

always around the next mood, the next
disquiet where dreams divide.

Facts and points of view intact, the work
within, the search both near and far,

back roads lead to knowing all the way
ahead to where and who you really are.

You Ask How
after "The Journey" by Mary Oliver

to grieve for the undead, the living gone
from you in your own growth. No one else
can say what must be entered into.
They may never come back or reach you

where you cannot compromise your honor,
your examined fears. You may move
mountains with prayers and tears but don't
count on moving any but your own. You may

try to meet them where they are. Be on guard.
They want you back to rage against, to keep
you tapping the dead familiar dance.
You may find their angst a vortex beyond

your endurance and need to close a door
to stay alive. There are no rituals for this
and most will never know. Take heart.
When you choose to trust and retreat,

you shift the coveted positions, realign love.
This voice can become your ally among
many you will make, the amazing gates
flung open when you least expect.

To Saint Francis

It's taken time to see how images
in your life mirror mine, both
enduring fathers who loved money

and goods more than self. You threw
down coins and cloth that filled the coffers
of his life, his daily bread that fed no one.

You stripped yourself of his ego, his claim
of father, refused to possess, rebuilt
your life brick by brick of resolve.

I have heard you in children's cries,
in the poor and disowned. You drew me
to the beauty of birds, the wild things

and woods, led me into a new way
of being in the world where once only
confusion prevailed. You taught me

to see and move on, be at home within.
Centuries can never erase your life,
your love, all the belittled lives you built.

Survivor

One dandelion in the lawn
eludes the hoe's sharp edge,

the stalk topped
with a cloud of seeds.

One swivel of morning air
is all the tuft

needs to usurp itself.
One by one, hair-thin strands

waft away like bee umbrellas
in the sun.

II. A Road Rarely Taken

Poetry is a sort of homecoming.
—Paul Celan

Arrivals

When some novel or simple idea slips
        into awareness, arrivals happen.
A scene or photo implodes
the mind with new insight: a person
whose name or face is unfamiliar, a home

        whose door opens to surprise,
an abandoned barn falling in on itself.
I arrive at deep notches in tips
        of chickweed petals, a fugue
of sand patterns on dunes, children dancing
        under blue and yellow umbrellas.

Arrivals lead me to unforgettable destinations:
a conversation with a stranger in a pub
        or park, a waiter interpreting a menu
at a German *Essplatz,* a crumbling bridge,
        a broken-down trestle.

Yet time is unpredictable, no promise
of what can happen once the instant appears.

Arrivals keep me alert, occur if I am ready
or not. Quick as a heart beat,
        gone in the blink of an eye.

The House in Hopkinton

It stands apologetic, the house where my two sisters
and I lived briefly after Mother died:
the stone porch with its magical swing, the chimney
covered with pigeon stains, French windows
smudged under dark-webbed eaves.

Behind the house, in the same barn where the Fiddler boys
snapped the necks of sparrows, a tenant woman sits
in a canvas chair sorting junk, stockings bagged around
her ankles. She greets us, then rambles on about the barn's
contents, the three-legged stool she squatted on for milking,

a plow and harness once attached to a single wagon tree,
forks for pitching hay, a rusty hoe. Pausing, she offers
to lead us to the house. Avoid the kitchen—too cluttered,
she says. From the front door, in resplendent litter
of the house, the barn becomes a pale reflection, every room

stashed with boxes, buckets of empty bottles and Mason
jars, spools of ribbon and string. Stacks of nineteen-forties
newspapers line a path to the living room where the woman
slumps into an oak rocker, speaks to my sister about books
on the dusty shelf, leaded glass and antique sales in town.

> Sitting beside the hearth in his favorite chair,
> my devoted grandfather pokers the dying coals
> into flames. His smoking stand holds matches
> he snaps as he cups one hand around his favorite
> pipe, the sweet aroma, perfect rings circling

our upturned heads. I taste after-dinner treats
under overturned plates, pull strings of the butterfly
lamp for a bedtime story, snuggle with my grandmother
on the piano bench as she plays "O Come Little Children,"
and sings in her alto voice. At naptime I climb

back stairs to a rag doll and darkened rooms, trace
circles with spit on the bedroom mirror. I shout
at the pigeons fluttering on hidden ledges of chimney
stones, smell fresh Kolach and coffee wafting
upstairs from the sunny kitchen.

I tap my sister on the shoulder, step to the porch into sultry air
and the unforgettable coo of a mourning dove.

As If We'd Walked Through Fire Together

In the backyard of my neighbor's house,
a face forms from corkscrew willow:
hair line and brows of twigs, the branch end's
dark eyes partially hidden by ferns.

My sister's features brighten in the sun's
slant as if wanting to know what she didn't
when she was alive, as if wanting to share,
eager to listen now that secrets no longer

exist. Now that walls of silence open as air,
we speak to each other, go back
to beginnings, unroll the unknowns, turn
the key to the unopened trunk with its secret

contents. Finally we gather the scattered
threads into bouquets of understanding
as if we'd walked through fire together
and come back singing.

When the sun slips, my sister's face
slowly flows into shadow. All that remains:
her receding eyes and laughter,
the sound as it fades.

Clara

plays the organ on Sundays
at the Bohemian church, then walks
across town and plays at late Mass

for the Germans. Summer evenings,
she gathers with sisters and brothers
on the family porch. Great Uncle Engle

pumps ivory keys on his accordion,
William whistles into tin, Hank hollows
his hand over a silver harmonica.

Great Aunt Kate bows her violin strings
and Wilbur clicks spoons on his knee
while Clara sings alto verses

with Anne, her soprano sister. Music
ripples over acres of corn,
over soybean fields, through elms

to neighbors' yards. Cattle stand still
as if astonished. Chickens scatter,
pigs cock ears. Songs and ballads

echo into evening. Laughter spins
through sunlight and shade until dark
descends and fireflies lower the stars.

The years roll on and still
this family imitates the sounds
from yellowing photos in an album

open on the table for everyone to hear.

Summer Days

In Grandma's front door oval window,
the beveled glass stallion offers its peaceful presence
during our visits to her home in a state away. After all
the greetings and directions to sleeping rooms,
the unpacking after a cold drink, time to unwind
from the long drive, we children begin to explore
back rooms and stairs, the tool shed behind the house.

A force pump outside the back door frightens us
when water comes gushing without warning though
the days are hot and splashing feels refreshing.

Every night after dinner, Grandma tosses the remains
in an iron pot and sends us next door to feed Mrs. Mendor's
ducks that waddle and run for the leavings. The neighbor
stands in the doorway and claps her hands in delight,
then wipes them on her white flour sack apron.

Grandma's low front porch is often empty on evenings
when the sun is hot so we gather chairs and a bench
in the shade. We take turns lying in the hammock Grandpa
strung between two sycamores. As the night wears on,
fireflies light the yard and we busy ourselves catching them
in Mason jars with holes poked in the lids.

Storms never come up while we stay at Grandma's
house though the cellar behind the house offers safety
if any funnel-shaped cloud appears in the distance.
It's the place for jars of canned peaches and pears, beans
and asparagus that line the shelves. On one hot day
we are allowed to open large double doors and follow
cobwebbed steps to the earthen floor, feel the cool air
surround us. Though it is dark and damp, it's an exciting
place to be. It offers safety from storms, but is not,
as Grandma warns, a place to play.

On Saturday afternoon, we walk the narrow sidewalk
with weeds between the cracks. Town is four blocks
to the movie theater for cartoon time or a Roy Rogers movie.
Sometimes we have an extra nickel or two for popcorn
but are careful to make our allowance last the week.

Some days we spend on the school playground swinging
over the bars, or backyards of our cousins' homes playing games
of tag or hide-and-seek. On some evenings before dark, all
the cousins gather to play kick the can or touch tag. Before
the final call inside, we run through last drops of the sprinkler
on grass that will wilt again by morning.

I especially remember the town clock and the chimes heard
from the highway and cornfields down the dusty roads.
On certain days, neighbors bring fresh-picked corn to the door.
That's when Grandma corrals us all into her kitchen to shuck
and pick silk from every ear for the evening meal.

The water tower adds its own fascination with large letters around
the tank's belly that spell *Dodge* where it can be seen for miles.
No one forgets the people who once lived there and now rest
in the Bohemian and German cemeteries at opposite ends of town.

Finally, the day arrives when our parents, aunts and uncles return
from the Southern Rockies and mountain peaks of Colorado.
With our bags ready, we sadly say goodbye to some of the best
days we would ever remember with cousins and Grandma waving
goodbye from the front porch. The years roll on and one day
a letter arrives that Grandma is very ill, so we gather again and tell
stories over and over with new takes and twists I never remember
happened—but all of it did.

A Road Rarely Taken
Nerinx, Kentucky Retreat

The road passes a barn. Beyond,
bales of hay lie in weeds,
rolled and wired. A fork in the road
offers a path to the hermitage,
or one to the lake. I choose the latter.

I think of the turn we took
thirty-five years ago when we left
our monastic lives and married.

Pebbles edge a narrow path
where wind spins the water. A sycamore
streaks arms of light in all directions.
I wait for the doe to come down to drink,
for its innocent face to tell me
there is nothing to fear.

Then, the road hairpinned up a mountain
as we forged through thickets
of resolve. It was the changing times,
challenges in the fresh air of openness.

Pin oaks, larch, bracken fern
border the lake. A leaf falls
from the maple where an empty branch
holds a barn wren pecking mites.
Water ribbons the rocks, reds and golds
across the lake as if I could ride them
down to their roots.
A hawk circles then disappears.
Grasshoppers fly from my feet.

We choose a divide that unites,
a break that bonds.
How far,
how near to know who we are.

Beyond low hills, a motor shatters
the silence. Tracks lead
to an empty house, paned door
and dark windows, stories still to be told.
Late afternoon I leave the lake,
the water tower that stares down the sun,
the road that returns to the fork,
the silo that holds itself in shadow.

Up Close
for AJM

Held together by a single pin, worn
leather swivels away to reveal two
spheres of glass. He stashes the magnifier
in a shirt pocket, useful when curious

about a book, a foreign stamp, a fragment
of bone. I observe him use it to enlarge print
from an old thesaurus, for lucidity in root
words of a Latin translation. He searches

for metaphysics of maps, ordinary objects
looking for candor, essence of honesty
in simple and complex ways of seeing.
He gathers the larger image of hours,

illuminates how matter matters in the great
pattern of the universe, how everything
observed enlarges perception, how a quest
burgeons insight. Always ready for new

revelations, every word, book, belief
augments and shapes his life. He amplifies
the moment, a clarity he approaches beyond
the lens and tattered leather cover.

The Clapboard House

sits on a bluff above the bay.
Somewhere a road leads to it
though it's impossible to see.

Giant cedars and brambles
surround the land. Sometimes
the windows flash gold at dusk.

From where I sit it seems
forsaken, an abandoned
dwelling one might come upon
in a tangle of overgrowth.

Yet, distant neighbors live there.
Smoke unfolds every morning
from the stone chimney,

sometimes swoops low depending
on the weather. Perhaps
someone stands at a window,
ponders my chimney swirls.

Perhaps that's all we need
to know, a home with someone
speaking in silent signals
that we are—and we are here.

Invisible Questions

Out for a morning walk, I slow where a young man
waters beds of Canterbury bells and cosmos. I
I pause to admire the blooming daisies
that have survived winter. He points to the mallow,
how hummingbirds sip from the cupped leaves

in summer. Then he pulls photos from a jacket pocket,
names flower clusters in his thriving garden: the green
mission bells mottled with yellow, splashes of rose
dianthus hugging the rock-ledge border. *The azaleas
died,* he confesses, *the roots wrapped in a ball,*

nothing but rock to reach around. The garden
raises invisible questions. I walk away nourished
by color and decay, by connection and conversation.
Denny says, *Come back for the dahlia flares
and coral flocks, for starters when the fuchsias rise.*

The Woman from India Who Lives Across the Street

Though her language eludes me, I learn to decipher her gestures, her tone of voice. I test my guesses one early spring morning as she is out for her morning walk, her white veil flowing over her shoulders in the brisk April wind. When she sees my *for sale* sign on the front lawn, she raises her arms, walks quickly toward me as I gather the morning mail, her words flying with a light rain just beginning to fall. When we meet in the middle of the street, we embrace as her words continue to flow. She points to the sign with questions and comments I can't decipher, but I know the message. We both remember the children, years of friendly encounters. Today, after her walk she reaches her porch, fumbles in her pocket then paces and gestures to me that her door is locked and she has no key. Bewildered, she crosses the street, gestures for the use of my phone. I invite her in, prepare tea while she calls her son, then hands me the phone as she breathes a sigh of relief. When her son arrives, she quickly crosses the street. From her front porch she smiles as her grandchildren do and holds up the key, happy to enter her home again.

Ahimsa Women

Franciscan Women
    Love in Action, Thich Nhat Hanh

An oval-shaped prism hangs
by a strand in the parlor window.
As the women gather in the silence
of Sandia foothills, a thimble of color
crosses the gray carpet, rainbows
for brief moments each dull tuft
of wool. It needles its way along
the sun line, over a table leg, a lap,
an arm of flowered chair, consumed
at the shadow's edge. The women

speak of healing a future ravaged
by war, voices of women and children,
undesirables stripped of respect.
Ahimsa women know the power
of no harm, the refusal of division,
the crescendo of awareness.

Answers surface inching light,
true colors of love, each woman
sensing a presence in every fiber
of desire, every thread of hope
for the future. This is the essence
of home, this hallmark of peace
where women honor their words.

In Bas-relief

1

On Novena nights, my childhood friend and I kneel
in the same pew at St. Ann's. Across the aisle,
a stained glass window opens to sultry summer air.
Above, a woman sits between stone columns
outside an upstairs window. She presses her smallest
finger against her lip, thumb on her chin bone, elbow
in her left palm. This third station-of-the-cross
unnerves me every Friday night. I see only
indifference in her pose, her eyes as she stares
beyond the scene below as if atrocities were trivial,
as if the stricken man bearing wood beams
did not create a crime against the world.

I wonder why she doesn't join the weeping women,
stand beside the brave, bloody her hands, chance life.
All I see is stone.

2

Years pass and now she speaks to me from the same
sill. *You question my intent, see only from your side.*
Here on this ledge soldier eyes follow my every move.
I pretend dispassion for this torn man in the screaming street
below whose last meal I served a night ago. I forgive your
judgments. The day will come for me to answer—and for you.

Hidden Mystics
  Monastery Retreat

This monastic chapel reflects a medley
of tenets. No figures of saints
      or rose design wedges,

only spaces and shapes of inherent mystics
lie hidden there. The Tao's praise of silence
      flows through ivory tint,

radical abandon like wind through hollows
      as the ordinary earns
honor in a vast empty place of no-knowing.

A Zen lamp of liberation shines. With mystical
acumen, Christ speaks in triangular shapes,
      all-loving presence,

lotus of the heart. A path of presence
      surrenders to fire
a blue background, Islam's flame,
a square panel in a gold vessel.

Through choral hue, Allah appeals for peace.
The Dharma sits in a triangular pane

at the edge of a sea wall, ponders the waves,
      a trickle of water down
from the mountain where Santor's stream

has no end. So many enduring rivers
surge through leaded glass, so many homes,
      so many beliefs flowing through light.

Sidewalk Artist
Port Townsend, Washington

A woman in jeans and red vest kneels
on the corner of Quincy and Water. Pastels
once boxed in rainbow rows lie worn
and scattered. She sits back on her heels
to see what she can't up close. The face

of a young woman brightens with mauve
and ivory sticks, the blouse blues and melon
greens, the ebony hair. You know the tourists
are awed by the way their mouths open,
by the almost inaudible sounds of soft *Ohs*,

by the raised eyebrows. The artist knows
before she begins, the face will fade, first rain
mottle the lines and spaces, colors run
at random and into each other, trickle down
alleys. She works with abandon, a degree

of detachment monks would envy. All
destined to the bay and beyond to the sea.
What remains from moment to moment: desire,
the pleasure of swirls and shades, shadows
and hues, stroke on stroke to completion.

Mahsi

She and Grandfather lived in a brick house
in a small town. The backyard a flower

garden where I watered her dahlias
and marigolds with my butterfly watering can.

Sometime we gathered red raspberries
and ripe tomatoes. Just to be near her,

just to feel the touch of her hand made me
feel whole and important as only a small child

could comprehend. After all these years,
I can still see the colored eggs scattered

over the lawn on Easter morning
and the peppermint sticks under our plates

as a surprise and smiles after loss no child
should know. She always wrapped me

in all the colored aprons of her love though
after Grandfather died, she moved away.

We stayed close over the years with letters
I hurried to open. She promised a spring visit

but became ill and after a few months she died.
After her funeral, we gathered at her grave

for one last goodbye. The threads of her love
wove a garment for me I wear every day.

Art Gallery Karma

On a glass shelf, a bronze Buddha reaches
with unopened eyes, outstretched arms,
        yet fully awake.

To stand before him spins my heart
        on its head. Inches away
perches an owl, its eye on the dark side

of life. Bronze figurines, collaborators
in unknowing ways, in the clarity of what is

and is not. They laugh and hoot at ideas
of excess worry carried as senseless weight.
        They scoff at being

or not being noticed when art lovers focus
attention on paintings, shimmering
        strands of jewelry, colorful scarves.

Lucent as lamps, they delight in dancing,
        flight in stillness, empty and full
in the place and moment they happen to be.

In the Optician's Waiting Room

Four women sit in silence at a circular table.
A thousand-piece puzzle provides a challenge

as they choose a shape, search, then set it
aside hoping to add a fit or two before

the time is up. They seem to know the act
of completion is not the point in these brief winks

of time. When Martha's name breaks the silence,
perhaps she dreams of reconciliation. Emily

rises, may wonder if her blurred vision will abate.
As Rita leaves, others fill the empty chairs.

It's possible the joy in her life is real and will last.
When I hear my name, I envision everyday shapes

of a complex world, the tests and attempts.
The challenge is mine, one wedge, one blink at a time.

Refuge
Mount St. Helens

                                    Ash
silvered the lawn for days. Warnings sounded,
voices spoke of danger. The blast burned acres

                of forest, lava flowed, everything
living lost in the rush. The sun darkened
with swirling plumes seen for miles, then winds
        carried them east.

             For months the mountain smoldered,
only thick gray adorning its flanks.
    Predictions—centuries would pass
before even a sprig of life reappeared.

What was not predicted—lees
    no larger than locust wings began to seep

                with light, seedlings and insects
inching into air. Now moss and fleabane cover
    the mountain that once raged with flames
            and thunder. Now nothing remains

of the chaos but swirling winds from the crater
        as if from a cabin chimney.

When loss threatens and ruin frightens,
        a haven appears to shelter ideas,
to imagine beyond, to know nothing
        can hinder the eruption of dreams.

Who Knows

Outside my window, the neighbor's
maple, only a scatter of hand-sized leaves
            left to fall.
It will take more lazy winds than these
      to release the last.

The fronds will find themselves
when rain and sun have done their work
to complete the art of surrender.

When the pruner arrives to strip
the tree to little more than a stump,
         everything happens
in the standing limb, in the hum of lawn,
              in the stark outlines.

How many seasons remain?
Why do I want to know when
        only unknowing knows?

III. A Wild Order

Going to the mountains is going home.
—John Muir

The Honey Work of Bees

If I could see with heron eyes,
count cells in a sandalwood chip,
or cups it takes
to fill a dune, if I could fathom
universe depths, distance

between stars, or imagine
the world in a pinpoint of earth, if I
could answer a kingbird,
or a shadow's silence,
I would know parts have power

to soften the riverbed, the peony air,
last rays of sun on the peach
before it falls.
As for the onion, who could question
the tissue-thin spheres

or the bottle fly's metallic blue?
If I could envision the moon
from its darkest surface, the sun's
fiery tongues,
or hear the murmur of wavering lights

dance over snow in a northern
night, then I would know the sea
and spirals of clouds
pursue their own destinations.
The skein of years unravels

in the blink of a minnow's eye.
In a breath, the whole appears
out of nowhere,
all bundled with intention
and the honey work of bees.

Even Pebbles

What abandoned the shell if not a life
that slipped from itself. Even pebbles

have something to say in silence.
We must speak for soundless things,

the zebra with stripes, the fawn with spots.
Even patterns on a mottled sea star, metallic

colors of mallard feathers, a lamp shell's
delicate shape deserve words. The art

of emptiness lies in a stone, the ornate
vase on a shelf as if a bowl full of answers

could be found in a drop of water or an ocean
of whelk. Every barnacle and brittle star

solicits questions. Yet answers may end stop
the quest. Only questions dangle

the carrot ahead, keep the kangaroo ready
to leap, the tortoise determined to win the prize.

Flycatcher

On nights of longing and memories,
      the forest bed fills my sleep
            with memories of pine.

A man sits under quaking
      aspen and calls in his quiet voice.
            Wake up, I'm the yew,

the heron, the river. I know you
      here in the heart of hills
            and oceans of sky.

Can you love me now in the ways I am?
      Can you find me in wild ginger,
            in the loon's cry?

Can you hear me in bells of nodding onion
      the flycatcher's song?
            I'm here in Alpine herb,

in the heart of the nootka rose.
      I'm wherever you are, the shadows
            that fall and the light.

      I'm awake I say—*I'm awake.*

In Celebration of Telephone Wires

They stretch for miles, those lines and spaces

waiting for the notes to arrive: black octaves

of grackles and crows, white-breasted nuthatch

and swallows. I arrive at dusk where the air

fills with a flutter of wings. The birds huddle

and the wires begin to sway. They are directors

and performers of their own renditions creating

a sold-out concert, an ensemble of sounds

only they can hear. Consumed with seeds

and berries, they gather after the work of feeding

and flight. So many measures they fold in their plumes.

We honor the lingering lines and spaces, the rests

and fugues before the wings fall away into night

or the tiny heads slip under feathers in sleep.

Between Cemetery Road and the Blue Tavern

two shadowed lanes curve
through Issaquah hills, past
faded horse barns, broken fences,
roads disappearing in dark
places the sun never sees. Yet
around one bend, sun slants

its slow winter splendor, bathes
a cedar grove in bronze, every bough
cast in metallic shine as if,
in the shutter of an eye, the moment
exposes, imprints on the day
another indelible presence.

Autumn Zen

...men loose, walking in the midst
of the fire and they have no hurt...
—Daniel 3:25

Witch alder's orange splays
across mountain slopes
with lemon of paper birch

and pin cherry red.
Leaves flutter the hills
like tanager flocks in flight.

Sun flickers an expanse
of color across
the mountains, a scene

no gallery can comprehend.
Leaflets twist, trust
the clusters they cling to,

un-busy themselves
from summer control,
age gracefully as a pasture

rose or moccasin flower.
Each hand turns in its own
time, content

in the red-brush wind.
Clusters spiral, linger,
and in the flutter of an eye

fall. From a distance, hills
and rivers blaze with quiet
flames like Shadrach singing

in euphoric fire.

A Wild Order

Dark holes, those empty spaces no eye
can see into, the kind a fallen cedar makes,
or a nurse log, its branches bent under ferns
and mouse-ear chickweed as if leisurely walking

a treadmill of wind. More than mice and spotted
beetles vie for the darkness. Even a ringed-eyed
raccoon slumps in the lush hollow.
The lichen will never bloom, nor moss clinging

to alders, fiddleheads of ferns. A slant of light
strikes the chopped wood stacked in a wagon,
the one beside a back door
as if someone delivered it to the woman

who peers between yellow curtains,
wanting to be sure. The deer nibble on thistle weed.
For a moment the sun seems hooked
on a cedar as it stitches its way into morning.

The spruce blues its smallest branches
when no one sees, the shy tick of the fox sparrow
choosing shadows. Everything
the way it is, chaotic order in the wild.

Woman Feeding Birds

Her tight body-shaped coat keeps out the wind
        as she scatters crumbs across the lawn.
With morsels still airborne, a singular language

speaks from every needle cluster
        every branch and alder limb. Flocks of gulls
and crows rise out of white birch and hemlock,

acres of spruce and cedar. They circle the green
        boughs, their wing tips streaks of sun. Hundreds
touch on the tawny grass long enough to grasp

the white bits in their beaks, scurry to steal
        what they can. Full of a life I know nothing
about, their presence tells me something

centers in the feathered breasts
        and cradled brains, something round like a halo
or an aura of ease. Are they apparitions,

beggars at the door to open the mind to more,
        the woman an angel in disguise?
Her seeds scattered, she turns and walks away.

Light slants and shadows weave,
        not a black, nor almond wing anywhere.

The Holly Tree

Some days the wrens are silent
as if they have lost their voices or flown
to a place where singing is always in the air.
They are rarely seen, sometimes
for days where they nest year around
in thickets of glossy leaves.

Other days when the sun is warm
and wind brushes their breast feathers,
musical chatter resounds up and down
the trails. It's as if something

in each tiny bird must rouse the world
to attention. All that's needed
is a listener or two. Though the roads
are empty, they go on for hours
chirping their hearts out,
depending on no one
to make a music only they can inspire.

Who will pick up the notes they leave
when darkness falls? Like mist,
bird song lingers in the air.

A Hammock

of web rocks between twigs
in a fallen pine, a spider
the size of a pea asleep in its center.
Like aphids and ants, the napper

knows what it needs. It waits
in shadows, savage as a wasp
when the hunt is on, stitches spaces

between stones and skirts
of cedar, snaring in and out
of the hours. An inchworm risks
its life by feigning death, the dragonfly

scoops bees in flight. These artful mites
surrounded by danger, lure prey
to the kill in the safety of survival.

Sandpipers

A spotted sandpiper pecks among
the beach stones, skips with twig-like legs

on seaweed and wood debris. I approach
in my red cap and winter coat,

note its head turn, the cautious eye keeping
a stone's-throw distance. It feeds alone

on sand fleas and elvers, skitters at random,
stares. I gather myself on a dry log

and soon a soft trill to my left, a clear
peet-weet rises from the olive-brown throat.

To my right, an echo down shore, calls,
caution in the shrill cries. When I first arrived,

the buff-colored bird foraged undisturbed
at the high tide line. Taking no chances,

answers whistle from its needle-thin throat,
and before I can blink, feathers hiss an arc

around me far out on the water, over
a flock of ducks and back where the pipers

join on the sandy rise and peck together
at broken shells and bits of shore crab.

Wood Path

A doe browses in a small clearing
of yellow weeds and pampas grass.
Soft rain dapples
her tan coat. She leads two
fawns no larger than spaniels,
pauses, ears alert, then bends
to the tansy leaves.

The fawns press at her side.
One stares when it sees me,
spots on the tawny
coat like snow. They munch
the mayweed, disappear

behind a hedge of nettles.
Two bucks appear from a cluster
of birch, follow the doe
to low-hanging leaves of honey locust.
They work their way along
the salal shrubs,
leave oleander and lamb's ear
untouched.

The deer drift so close
I can see light in the onyx dark
of their deft eyes—mountain
lakes and a crescent moon.

Salt

From a distance, pygmy poppy heads
and dune tansies toss on hairy stems.
Closer, wind ruffles the tissue wings of six

yellow butterflies rippling to a niche
of wet sand. They seem out of place,
no woods, no savanna, no milkweed

for miles; they seek grains for the long
migration to meadows of wild plum
and passion flowers. For the moment

they have found their centers,
content to sip the sweetness of salt.
They rise together, then descend

dropping again and again to savor
the moist sand. Sun scatters gold
on the water, and still they rise

and fall. When the crests are limned
with moon and tides fill cowry hollows,
their wings will rest on a coil of kelp,

or begin the migrant journey south.
Imagine such fragile command,
such daring so close to thunder.

In Praise of Skunk Cabbage

Water quickens under the bridge,
near the pond where the gray-green algae

begins to fade. Beyond the stone arch,
the cabbage with their yellow hoods

and flowered horns announce spring,
candles flaring among the bracken

and beige scraps of knotweed. Soon,
chameleon-like, they will shift colors

to the cocklebur and tarweed's deep green.
Now they are lanterns in the swamp

among the clumps of tawny slough,
whose luster will linger long after

the feathery spindles of grass die back
and the elephant leaves decay.

The Pond

I part thick alder canes, thistle clusters,
brambles of yellow pepper weed until I stand
at the water's edge where the surface
        lies still as morning dew. What appears
as slivers of dawn from the narrow trail
becomes a blanket of haze over broken branches,

elm and willow. Water partially hides an abandoned
water wheel. Floating mosquito ferns and bushy
        pondweed undulate in mist.
Phragmites and purple loosestrife reflect
                from the opposite bank.

The sun slowly spreads day over the surface,
a seam sewn between opposites, dark underworld,
light separations. On the far side, cordelia calls
        of a hermit thrush,
unexpected voices of a gray catbird mimic
rock wrens, winged teal. Fronds of sword ferns
            waver in morning's warmth.
A bog turtle suns on a broken snag. A bell frog
slips like vague speech under the pond's rippled surface.

Suddenly from seclusion the white plume feathers
of an egret rise, in moments disappear,
        leaving a clear blue river to flood the sky.

Snow Goose

The snow goose glides
backwaters of the pond.
Pigeon-gray patches of sky

mirror her fading wings. Soon
she will be white as reflections
of the snow-covered mountain

rippling beside her, rising
among tangles of brush,
vast ranges
of cedar and birch. At night,

the snow goose nests
near the salmonberry, morning
light slips in and out
of the pond with fog
or hovering caps on the summit.

Sometimes the mountain
may disappear
as if it had never been. Nothing

is ever far from extinction.
Nothing certain what the day
will hold. What's seen from any
perspective still shines despite
the dark when the snow goose

sleeps, at home near the heron
with bedstraw swirls, the sweet-
scented blooms of bog orchid.

For What They Are

Evening arrives. Driftwood, sand dollars,
polished stones stipple the shore we walk.

Memory pools possessions; cowry sensing
the way it sees the world, the glossy

shell a protection, implicit will to survive.
Trails ripple across the sand: clam,

periwinkle, fluted limpets. The ocean gathers
gifts, decor or detritus: sea lettuce, kelp,

eelgrass, feathers—everything lustrous
with sunset fire—hollows in beach rocks,

edges of thunderous crests flush
with evening's last flare. We linger for the sun

to drift below the sea, for the ascendant
dusk slowly to yield its polished moon.

Mount Rainier

A presence over valleys and high
ridges, an unseen pebble skipping
Mowich Lake. Cap clouds over the mountain

remain the climate of legends, capture
the eye for miles. When the clouds descend,
a wall of mist deceives, a magician's

empty hand. Permanent snowfields,
glacier caves all dissolve; massive
cedars, acres of avalanche lilies

vanish in the wind. When the mountain
disappears, invisible fires
burn in the mantled heart.

In Ragged Tide Waters

a periwinkle shell lies unbroken,
rings winding to a tiny center,

a delicate sheath exposed
in the surf at low tide. It weighs

no more than a feather,
beads of morning dew long dried.

The tawny eye looks up at me
as if I should know the root

of its lucent texture, or fathom
the ebb and flow of giving

and receiving a pattern of living with
and without.

I stoop to inspect but not retrieve.
It belongs to the sand

and the sea, this shell a universe,
a mirror of itself, a search

for something beyond the touch.

Woods Near Lake Elysian

      On the leaf mold path to the lake,
scraps of twigs touch and bend, swirl
and sigh with the easy wind. Splinters

      of sun weave through the woods.
In a thicket, three elms form an *O*
of absence, a somber tone of emptiness.

These codes of wholes and parts catch
      my breath, offer a bittersweet brief
understanding. Later, a full moon rises,

an undivided ring of light. My eye
refuses division: omega sparks on the lake,
      sycamore's rotund shapes,

the barn owl's eyes from the aspen.
There all along, signs the wind records,
      meant to remain and be remembered.

More Than

A ratty fist of weeds, not a bouquet
to be chosen for its color

and beauty though on a closer look,
yellow rays flower from the head,

one opening bud, another
sun-kissed bloom. Like notes

on a staff, there's a song somewhere
along the line moving up,

the falling back that happens:
the bend, the breaking, the inching into

under odds. Those highest tones,
tiny parachute seeds drift off

with the slightest breeze,
lightest breath full-blown and away,

a final burst to fulfillment.

IV. The Country of Home

Everyday is a journey and the journey itself is home.
—Matsuo Basho

Away

> *When you are everywhere, you are nowhere,*
> *when you are somewhere, you are everywhere.*
> —Rumi

To begin the journey, prepare.
Speak to friends, some who know.
Read about cities, customs, dark pages
      of history, people:
cyclists and pedal boaters stowing
      umbrellas on canal boats, naked
children playing in a Karlovy Vary
wading pool, shirts whipping from boat
      fish lines on the Mekong,
the taste of sweets from Han's bakery shop
a town clock ringing above
Groningen Square, water singing over
Tepla river rocks, synagogue walls
      covered with names burning
with dates of birth and death.
Yet knowing remains in books
and hearsay. The senses produce a place
      for the body to arrive
at the moment of meaning.
No boundaries exist except the created.
Now only the silent cries of the slain,
      the scent of smoke,
the floating oil from sunken ships
the parting of a curtained window,
      a swivel into light,
instant welcome at a wide open door.

Returning Home
to Vietnam
for Timothy

He sits next to me in the window seat.
Patches of land between clouds, memory
of a flight taken more than twenty-five
years ago: the rush, the confusion,

the choices, though only by hearsay
until he was old enough to know.
He says he feels a certain anxiety,
a strange feeling of returning to a home

he doesn't remember, people or places,
yet one that lives in his bones. His thoughts
uncertain, he leans to look again
and again to wings cutting the air to atoms.

Sky darkens and blurs into dusk.
He turns on the light, reads the story
of his arrival, a journey from where he first
inhaled the world, effects of war

he hopes won't follow him into the future.
For now he cannot know the beginnings
that await: his people, customs, land
he will come to love, friends waving

to him from sampans and bikes loaded
with mangoes and fish for the market.
Soon he dozes, dreams of what he may fear
and what will soon open his eyes to wonder.

Feasts on the Mekong Delta

From Saigon, we depart for Vinh Long, then
transfer to a cruise boat through small winding
canals, orchards lush with April fruit, a feast
of pomegranates, papaya and mango.

In a handcraft village, natives smile, happy
to see our smiles returned. We feast our eyes
on wall hangings with rainbow colors of yarn
and strands of silk. The young artists weave
intricate designs with a sense of home
and pride written on their determined faces,
honored to share their best selves
with strangers whose country once chose war.

We lunch with a bonsai gardener, enjoy
home-made rice wine. He offers a feast
of squid, spring rolls with shrimp and steamed
rice cakes. After the main courses,

three musicians arrive to entertain with zither,
drum, four-string guitar, a feast of music
where the evening swelters with song
and an enduring desire for peace.

An Dinh Palace

            The Heavenly Pagoda
hovers over the Perfume River, great
protector of dragon boats and people
ferried across the waters.

            Moon glistens
the rippling path, the motor thrumming
its way to shore. When it arrives
at the palace, we vest in silken robes
and hats despite the sultry heat.

            It is a festive night,
a ten-course meal, one adoptee the queen,
another, emperor, ruling above the dining
hall, surveying the friendly subjects.

            Hundreds of years
have passed since the hall was filled
with monarchs and nobles while peasants
dined from bamboo plates, cups of tin
and spoons.

            Yet even in huts
the people sing, musicians play on moon
lutes and zithers. There is dining on streets
from abundance in trees and garden plots.

            Strolling the lanes,
light from colorful lanterns abounds and all
the flickering candles.

Topiary

The green dragon bush kept
in shape by the keeper's shears

appears on a narrow flowerbed path.
A totemic animal, the dragon shows

itself etched in immortality, a symbol
of deity-clouds, rain for rice fields,

orchards and gardens. Here no incarnate
spirit of evil prevails, only signs

and symbols, care for the people, one
with peace and protection. We muse

on ways the world's events express
what words alone cannot, like

Enola Gay and incineration, grips
of terror ripping away the unwarned.

Let the body show how to shape,
the mind and will to shear divisions.

Souvenirs

As we gather near the pagoda
on the shores of the Perfume River,
a boat arrives to ferry us
to an ancient imperial palace. Peach
and dragon flowers, chrysanths
and marigolds scent the air. On walls

and posts, paper lamps and orchids
glisten in the genius of slanted light.
Sun fans the water gold.

Lavender pinks mark the mountains,
silky pastel colors at dusk shine
on the hills, a scene of souvenirs
to tuck away like a photo
encased in a gold locket.

These moments fit in the space
of a thought and when we leave
they turn like pages of a river flowing
into the past—and always present.

Ebbingstraat
Groningen

The restless days of rain finally relent.
Clouds nod past the sun as if apologizing.

In the narrow street, people saunter, stones
soften under their steps. Mothers pack children

in purple strollers, smiles appear out of dark
doorways. Bearded men rest on iron benches,

feed crumbs to pecking pigeons. In sunlight,
ruffling feathers silver. The herring mart and town

square fills. Bakery, *beukeveld*, apothecary
storefronts freshen as cyclists and pedal boaters

stow black umbrellas. Roofs glisten, reflections
ripple in canals, light enters lace-drawn windows

the way the people express themselves
in leisurely events from sun up to sun up.

Under a Prague Moon
for AJM II

Our son escorts us to the gate
of the first pension on U Lucie Street.
Light falls from lace-curtained windows.
Branches laden with peaches bend
to grass. The host, Jan, cups fingers
to his forehead, squints at the plump
flesh ripening. He hands me two
and takes us to tour his garden, tomorrow's
breakfast tomatoes, strawberries,
long rows of hidden *okurka*, some
for pickling. Giant dahlias shadow the lawn,
dill taller than a man. Brutus, the neighbor's
German shepherd, barks.

•

Carl, the Bohemian man on Vysehrad
Street speaks broken English.
His wife, Mira, fills cracks
in conversation. We are welcomed:
marquetry mums on the foyer's wall,
pelt of a chamois, a carved stein
on the pine shelf. Roses
in a cut-glass vase scent a writing table.
Between stems, a taupe spider wavers,
snatches dust specks to stay alive.
We open the blinds to a grove of *abliko*,
apple trees still tart green. Saturday
morning slips into blue. Carl tell us
the people are celebrating six liberated
years. Ivy geraniums spill over the window
box. This August they flush fullest pink.

•

In the Victoria neighborhood
the hostess welcomes us, serves Kolach
and guava juice on a shaded porch.
Ola cries at naptime, whispers into sleep.

A bucket of block toys
rests beside the umbrella table,
colored rope swings in the breeze.
Inside the house, a child sings.
Mila opens the screen door, shyly
shows us her kitten.
In a park, a man announces
unfamiliar scores from a soccer field

•

The last night we return to U Lucia.
Sun sets in a lilac sky.
We sip *becherovka* with our son,
taste one more time
wine made sweet under cellar stairs
where dark bites deeper than cold.
We toast time together, hosts and homes
resilient citizens in a city alive
after years of passivity. They honor
tourists with fruits of their work:
handmade figurines and flowers,
lace attire, pashmina scarves.

Outside, the melons round
the white-fenced rows, pea vines ready
for the morning pick. Our days
have plumped and ripened like peach-filled
limbs below our window. We pose
for pictures. Before sunrise,
we slip through the iron gate. Under
a Prague moon, tiled roofs brighten.

Art Gallery

A disk seen on the skyline
        at dusk, an opulent platter,
a crimson plate of plenty.

Flickers in fused glass
        scatter in gallery glow,
invite onlookers to a lavish feast
        of fire and abundance
igniting flames and fervor
        in those who hunger for light.

At a Kiosk in Prague Square

We tour the city, the magic of the square.
A puppet with an orange checkered hat
and a bulbous nose, hangs from a t-bar,
a wooden clown swaying in shade
like a live entertainer. He wears oversized
shoes and baggy trousers, twirls on strings
in the sultry air, the red-lipped mouth
upturned. I purchase the wooden artiste
to dance for my students on a painted stage.

I recall a recent circus where a live clown
carries a heart beneath the polka dot shirt,
a trickster, a performer who tries his best
to make people happy. Yet under the patches
and purple hat, he hides sadness and grief
in a pantaloon pocket, lets children know
life is more than what they see. No matter
what distress falls on their days, they can
pretend to the world—but never
to themselves.

When the clown returns to his home,
he empties his broken heart and down-turned
face until the ache subsides, the scar softens
to a memory and in a moment, he sees
another side of himself he grows to love. Then
he becomes the funniest clown in the circus.
Even dancers bouncing on balls, the trapeze
artist and the man who walks on stilts feels
the about-face. The circus goes on and on
in a tent where clowns are people with hearts.

When I return to my classroom and students,
the puppet from the kiosk in Prague
dances from strings and wakens delight
as children learn from the circus
the world of the whole human race.

Ghetto Cemetery

We walk among the dense stones,
a haunting place half a millennium old.
Here the bones of twenty thousand
Jews once enfleshed in the first ghetto,

lie in twelve layers of soil, their tombs
sprinkled with prayers on torn paper,
pebbles to hold them in place.
The headstones' Hebrew runes

and family inscriptions have crumbled
to sand, words whipped by centuries
of wind. Stone slabs lean
against each other like the dead

in camps of suffocation
packed into stacked graves.
On the south side, synagogue walls
burn with dates of birth and death

culled from Nazis' transport files,
floor to ceiling carved
and re-carved, hands still grooving
their story in stone. Out of nights

darker than the heart of rock,
the dead rise from ash
like gulls forever in flight,
feathers trusting the rush of wind.

Karlovy Vary
Czech Republic

We wander the mosaic streets where naked
children play in wading pools,
and guests ponder the curative powers

peace
holds over the people. Between colonnades
and gabled roofs,
water sings over rocks on the Teplá River.

The Czech spa town appears at the end
of winding chestnut groves.
A city

discovered in a moment they say
by the howl of a scalded hunting dog,

an exposure made famous for its hot
springs and cures, a city
noted for its poets,
writers and composers,

a place many call home
where cherry blossoms thrive.

On a Train from Padua to Venice

It sounds like background music
from the train speakers, but when

the car door opens, a small boy leads,
holding a tin can in his outstretched hand.

Behind him, a boy about ten follows
slowly down the aisle, his fingers spilling

over the keys and pumping pockets of air
from his shiny accordion. His face beams

as if certain of acceptance. Or is it a mask
he hides behind, a child laboring

for handouts? For a moment
passengers look up from their papers,

then go back to news of births and deaths,
weather and wars. I'm captivated

by "O Sole Mio" but when a first coin
clinks near the exit door and the pair

disappears from our blue compartment,
I know I have missed the moment.

He goes on playing from car to car
as if his life depends on it,

as if a response doesn't matter,
or matters immensely.

Pigeons Roosting on Ledges of the Bank Building and Loan
Groningen

We choose a table
looking down on the market square.
       Flocks of pigeons peck
the tan bricks clean

of bagel crumbs, croissant flakes,
       fruit bits.
Cyclists ignore the dull feathers
flapping around their feet.

       The beggar birds ascend
after feeding, seek rest

on ledges above the ornate pillars.
       From a third-story window
we notice two gray doves
tuck their heads under wings,

the life below irrelevant.
They have each other, a place
       in the world away,

the owl-like calls, olive-buff eggs,
black darting eyes closed in sleep.

Poor Man
Assisi, Italy

All I had was hearsay, impressions
of pilgrims. In grass overlooking
hillside maples and rooftops,

I sense his voice in the wind, music
he heard in olive trees, his elation
like waters leaping down falls.

He dared to stand against dishonor,
build walls of candor and rooms
of compassion. Spirits still reside

as wings in the shadowed alcoves fold
at dusk and lift when light scarlets
the dawn. Places he rode, the ancient

Umbrian way on his travels to Florence
or Rome, over peaceful countryside,
mirror-like waters reflecting morning sun.

Valleys appear where he rebuilt his world,
spent hours in pastimes and prayer,
transformed his life in fine disarray.

I can return again and again
where fingers of oak sketch his name
in the sky and fields cradle roots

of his fervor, where Francis loved all creation,
left his dreams to the least and the lost,
where he learned the secret of surrender.

From One Instant Reflection to the Next

The quiet lobby. Soft Japanese music seeps
        through ceiling speakers like morning mist.

A small clock on the window ledge scatters rainbow
        colors that brighten the reception desk

with luminous shades. Outside the lace-draped window,
        cars streak by in British patterns. Soon our son

will give us words for ancient temples and shrines
        as we once gave him words for rain and water

when he was without words, a guest in an unfamiliar
        world who draws us now into tea rose art

and tapestry weavers. Generations exchange
        courtesies like men in the lobby bow to each other

before and after business. One deed begets another
        long after images pass, long after colors

fade into shadow. Time rushes on like trains
        to another arrival, one instant reflection to the next.

Town Clock

Chimes ring through walls
      and high windows
           of fifty-seven Ebbingstraat.

Above Hans Optical shop,
      I can hear the soft hammer
           of the town bell tower

measure time of our home stay.
      Second to second, minutes
           swing through our days

like ticks of the clock sweep the coffee shop
      and bakery sweets, bicycle
           bells reliable as mothers

strolling infants, or fish peddlers
      shouting prices. Instants
           ornate our lives. Wheels

and cogs click increments of bustling canals,
      museum walks, buses
           and tour boats until

the moment arrives and the carillon bells ring over
      tiled roofs, through our decorated door
           to tell us the town clock

is always on time. We pack the hours,
      all the moments and memories,
           full circles of fading chimes.

A Home to Remember

The last day here, this one
dreamed, a home surrounded
by woods, open to doors
books no longer live behind,
a hearth where fire
no longer burns.

Packers seal boxes.
I think of morning voices
and sun rushing in,
white blossoms
on the Yoshino cherry,
birds swaying on feeders,
a hawk's wing
as it disappears behind
swaying skirts of cedar.
I remember the bonsai
pine, the monk
who sits under in silence.

This country of home
I hold here with you, the place
arrived in so many warm
and radiant rooms.

Answers

I find them in folds of my grandmother's
skirts, in songs sung around the piano,
family chorus flowing over the corn

and soybean fields. They can be found
in bonds of aunts and uncles,
cousins who know the meaning of fun

and laughter and offer it gladly though
they know nothing of me. Questions
find answers on some of the best

summer days when Grandma opens
her arms and heart to a house full
of children. I find them on my deceased

mother's palette: vibrant colors of finch
and peacock, country shanty along
the creek—her faded sheets of music.

I find answers where pygmy poppy
heads toss on hairy stems and sun
bathes a cedar grove in bronze.

They arrive when the doe and her fawns
nibble in the orchard, where yellow
butterflies dip again and again

to the moist salt, sand dollars stipple
the shore. Answers arrive on the other
side of the world where trains rush

from one illumination to the next,
where the town clock sounds
its bells to tell it is time
to fling doors open and stand beside

the forsaken. These are the doors
to the homes I inhabit. These are answers
to every question I've ever asked,
now to be home in the heart of homes.

Lasting

What love can do and be,
all the layers of it

like flames between mirrors,
the endless light,

endless expanse
of beauty and being,

a peaceful river
running away forever.

ABOUT THE AUTHOR

Kay Mullen spent the majority of her adult life teaching grade school children. After receiving a Master of Education from Seattle University, she became an elementary school counselor, working with children, parents, and school personnel to set the stage for success, not only in grade school but also in later school and adult life. After her work in the schools, she became a certified mental health counselor.

Kay later earned a Master of Fine Arts from Pacific Lutheran University with a focus on poetry. She received a First Place in the Washington State William Stafford Award and was a Best of the Net nominee as well as a multiple Pushcart Prize nominee.

Her more current work includes teaching poetry skills at Catherine Place, a center for women in Tacoma, Washington that fosters lifelong learning and leadership skills. In 2016, Kay edited an anthology of poems by Catherine Place poets: *Women Writing: On the Edge of Dark and Light*. Over the years, she has offered poetry workshops to various groups including both men and women in prison and those in transition.

Looking back on her writing she states: "I realize I intuitively strove to follow my birth mother's music and artistic gifts, somehow weaving them into my poems. My mother left me a legacy I discovered long after her death. She has become alive again in my poetry."